The Response
Cold E[

by

Josef Reisz

This Sales Pocket Guide is a concise, easy-to-read book that will help you get more business.

It's the only pocket guide sales book that shows you how to design a cold email that will get your prospect to respond to you

This book will explain the important structure of a great cold email:

1. *Subject Line*
2. *Addressing your prospect*
3. *Trigger Events*
4. *The Opening Line*
5. *Your Value Proposition*
6. *The Closing*
7. *Your Signature*
8. *PS:*

About Josef Reisz

Josef Reisz is a CEO with over 25 years of experience in the development of new markets, strategic planning and implementation.

Josef has been on both sides of the table; as an Entrepreneur, he started out by founding six successful companies, such as VU Capital, JRC Strategic Business Advisory and, most recently, HoneyComb Agency.

He also has extensive experience working for Fortune 500 corporations as well as smaller privately owned businesses - holding various roles such as Head of Sales, Marketing and eCommerce.

Josef Reisz is a serial entrepreneur with an impressive track record. He has had experience in various roles on the C- and Board level held positions as Head of Sales, Head of Marketing, Head of Ecommerce, CEO, Non-Exec and Advisory Board member.

Josef has written five books on topics ranging from personal growth to business success. His writings have helped countless people build better lives while growing their respective brands or companies.

About HoneyComb

HoneyComb is A Team Of Creative Strategists Who Love Crafting Beautiful, Smart And Inspired Strategies That Help Businesses Meet Their Most Ambitious Objectives.

HoneyComb provides In-Depth training with a proven track-record for sales organisations that enables them to hit their targets, stay motivated and incentivised, close more deals and generate more, predictable revenue for your organisation. Fast.

Fast-track Transformation of Organisations And Teams Into Well-Oiled, Homogenous And Inspired Powerhouses By Strategic Design.

www.HoneyCombAgency.co.uk

HONEYCOMB

Introduction

Cold emails are a crucial part of any marketer's toolkit, and they can be really effective when used well to get your foot in the door. But how do you know that you're writing a cold email that will get the desired response?

This book gives you valuable insights in how you can draft your cold (or warm) emails that piques your prospect's interest and will provoke a response from them.

There are techniques that you can apply that will increase your chances of getting your prospect to reply - sometimes within an hour(!) - of your outreach email. I will discuss these techniques with you in detail in this edition of The Sales Pocket Guide.

Format

- *No more than 90 words*

- *One sentence = one line*

- *No links (unless you provide valuable information as explained below)*

- *End with a 'next step'*

Every day, the amount of emails sent is incredibly high. Latest research shows that roughly 191 billion emails are sent daily. Because of this, you have to be efficient in every way possible and your email is one of the ways where you can do just that.

In order for someone to open up an email, they need to be interested right away or within the first 2.5 seconds. Latest studies have shown that this is exactly the time you have to get an Executive's attention in their inbox. What does that mean for you?

It means that your 'From' field and 'Subject Line' need to be ab-so-lute-ly spot on!

In a nutshell

- *Keep it short - no more than two sentences at most*

- *Include relevant information about who they are (e.g., company name, recent news articles), what kind of product/service they provide, and why this matters*

- *Mention their customer base (if applicable; e.g., "you have an audience of X,XXX")*

- *Be specific and show that you've done your research on them (e.g., mention a project they're working on)*

- *End with a clear call-to-action*

- *Make it as tailored to the prospect and their business as possible*

- *Research the business before hitting the 'Send' button*

- *Pique interest by referring to elements of their business, i.e. Trigger Events, or their personal involvement, i.e. keynotes*

- *Avoid mentioning your business / company name in the body of the email. Keep it to the signature.*

- *Never start your email with 'Re:' - This is highly deceiving if you haven't had a prior email conversation with your prospect.*

The Structure of your Cold Email

Every email has certain, repeating elements. These elements represent your cold email's structure. Knowing these elements will help you create cold emails that are more effective and help you save time in the long run.

Every cold email from a salesperson can be broken down into several parts.

Once upon a time, cold-emails were cold-hearted, cold-call scripts that salespeople directed at random people on the internet with no attempt to personalise their message.

But cold emails have evolved since then into a structured email that has:

1. *A greeting of some sort*

2. *An explanation of what this cold email is about (and how it can help them)*

3. *A sign-off of some sort*

4. *An opportunity to reply or take the conversation forward*

To make it more precise, we are now taking a look at the formal structure of a cold email. It is important to pay utmost attention to every part and not dismiss any of them as 'less important'.

Because every part is equally important for your cold email success.

Email Structure

1. Subject line

2. Addressing the prospect

3. The opening line

4. Your Value Proposition

5. The Closing

6. Your Signature

Knowing this structure, which should be common knowledge, is a start. But we won't stop there. Every piece of the structure is vital to your success. And making a mistake in any of these can dramatically damage your success. So let's start with the cold email's structure and break it down.

The Subject Line

The subject line of your sales email is the most important element because that is the first thing your prospect sees. Your subject line is the deciding factor for your prospect whether or not to open your email or delete it.

That's the only 2 options your prospects will grant you.

That's why you need to make sure that your subject line is relevant and specifically tailored to your prospect, and give an interest-piquing preview what the email is going to be about.

Relevancy, specificity and a straight-to-the-point approach will help you avoid the "I'm sick of all this spam" reaction that people have nowadays and it'll make your email stand out from the armada of desperate sales people.

When it comes to subject lines, personalisation is considered a must these days. If you want to be taken seriously by busy professionals like CEOs or other VPs of companies, adding their title (Mr., Mrs.) and name is not enough anymore. You need to prove that you've done your research about them and know how they're connected to the topic of your email.

This does not necessarily mean to put the prospect's name in the subject line. That looks...you guessed it, spammy.

Keep the subject line short, simple and straight to the point.

The more tailored the email is, the higher your chances to get a response.

The subject line is like the appetiser of your email. It needs to hook your prospect in, and make them want to open your email and read more. Because cold emails require effort and time from your end as well as from your prospects, they expect that an email they receive has something important or valuable for them.

Subject Line Topics

1. *Leverage a Trigger Event*

2. *Provide Value / Information*

3. *Use a Referral / Introduction*

4. *Ask to Identify Decision Makers within their organisation*

5. *Getting Results*

Now that we have taken a look at the different topics for your subject line, we can put that into action.

Examples

- *Your LinkedIn post yesterday*

- *Your keynote at XYZ…*

- *Your Blog*

- *Via LinkedIn - XYZ (if you have already connected with your prospect on LinkedIn)*

- *XYZ suggested to get in touch*

- *Question about COMPANY's growth strategy*

- *Your recent funding round*

- *Congrats*

- *One-Word Power Subject Line (such as: Growth, Sales, Strategy, Question, ...)*

Trigger Events

In order to make your cold email as tailored as possible it is imperative to do your research on your prospect and their business.

Trigger Events are your way into the organisation and in front of the decision makers, i.e. your prospects. If you do not have a pre-existing relationship (such as a contact, colleague or even LinkedIn connection) then cold emailing based on Trigger Events will help you get your foot in the door and convincesyour prospects to give you valuable time - if you go about it clever enough…

Utilising Trigger Events in your subject line and/or body of your cold email shows the prospect that you've done your homework, that he is not just a data entry in your CRM.

'Show me you know me' is a powerful tactic to build rapport in a sales call. Trust me when I say, building rapport in an email is equally important, yet much harder to accomplish. Trigger Events are a great way to get your cold email read

When cold emailing based on Trigger Events you want to assess the following:

- *Which companies have needs for your offering, given your knowledge of their industry?*

- *Where are they within their Decision Journey Map?, e.g. which stage are they at and what objections might they have?*

- *What makes them more likely to buy than other companies that you cold emailed?*

- *Do they fit your values and business ethics (a point that is oftentimes underestimated or ignored, especially with sales organisations that are desperate to close any customer)*

Trigger Events can be internal - within the business - as well as external. Internal trigger events are things such as an internal blog post, a recent product launch or rebranding, newly launched products etc. External Trigger Events are things such as awards won, mentioning by another company in the press, a well-known customer (of the prospect) choosing their competitors etc.

Examples

- *Annual Result reports*

- *New strategic directions*

- *Changes in Headcount*

- *Political changes*

- *Regulatory changes*

- *Economic changes*

Addressing The Prospect

Once you've written an amazing subject line and got it passed through A/B testing (you should do that by the way), the next step is addressing your prospect in a personal way.

It sounds obvious that cold emails should be addressed to someone specific, but only about 20% of cold emails are personalised, according to Experian data. This is why cold email response rates range from 1,2% to 7%

Now, before we get started, I'm going to ask you to forget what your parents told you: To always be polite and say "Dear Mr", or "Dear Mrs'.

Executives nowadays have very little time for that.

So here's how I do it:

Simply start with your prospect's first name in the first line of your cold email, followed by a comma:

John,

That's the best formula for keeping it formal and simple. Fair enough, if you know your prospect and have had conversations prior, it is absolutely OK to lead in with 'Hi FIRST NAME,'

Remember

If you want to be taken seriously, using an email address that is not tailored specifically for this particular person is a major faux-pas.

Be especially careful when you're addressing someone from a different culture than yours.

By the way, "Dear Sales Department" or not adding any name will never cut it as an opening line, just saying..

A simple "Hi (first name only)" or "First Name Only' will do the trick in most cases, even if it's not 100% polite, as we all have learned the societal principles of having manners. In this case, a cold email outreach, it is absolutely fine.

Please don't use '*Hey,*' unless you are close friends with your prospect. At least not in the initial outreach stage.

Emails are short and should be to the point. Think of them as being one or a few paragraphs long

So instead of writing a novel, write only what is necessary to get your message across. No more than 3 sentences and 90 words in total is a good indicator. This way your email will not seem desperate for attention and you are more likely to get a foot in the door.

The Opening Line

Your opening line of your cold email must be spot on, straight to the point and relate to a Trigger Event, either of your prospect or their organisation.

Why is that important?

You made it over the first hurdle: Getting them to OPEN your cold email. Now is the time to be intriguing and invaluable to them. They will be reading your email, because they are interested in the Trigger Event you mention. The reason why you send this cold email is to make a connection between their Trigger Event and what you have to offer them or how you can help them.

Hence, researching the company and the prospect is essential for your success.

With your email, you will want to either refer to an internal or external Trigger Event or simply provide value by sharing a relevant article or piece of content.

What to avoid?

Do not write cold emails that are very generic. A cold email is a cold call's electronic version.

As cold calls are irritating for most people, cold emails are also an unwelcome interruption in their day and they will be annoyed if the cold email does not have any relevance to them

You should take some time before sending your cold email and craft it with great care. If you do this properly, your prospects will appreciate your perseverance, dedication and individual approach

Why perseverance?

Studies have shown that it takes an average of 9 touch points with your prospects (via email, direct messages, emails, voice mails, etc) before sales people will get a response.

It is, therefore, important that you craft each message from you to your prospect with utmost care and be persistent in your efforts to get the desired outcome: A response.

If you want to increase your chances of success, use personalisation (to the extent which is possible). It forces you to do research about each person on the receiving end of your cold email.

Remember

The goal of your cold email is to get prospects interested enough so they request more information or reach out for an introductory meeting with you. In order for them to do that, you need to convince them of three things:

1. *You deserve their attention*

2. *You deserve their time*

3. *You deserve their business*

You can do that by providing value in your cold email or, even better, introducing them to a problem they need solved and how you want to help.

Examples

- *I just came across an article that said ...*

- *I just read your interview in XYZ where you mentioned your company's plans to expand your operations by 35% over the next 18 months*

- *XYZ just gave me your email because he/she thought you might be interested in what we've done in other companies in the XYZ sector*

- *Congratulations on how your firm performed in the past year. I was just reviewing your annual reports.*

- *I thought you might be interested in this new white paper on how to cut costs from your operations by 32% while adding 27% on average to the bottom-line*

Your Value Proposition

In your cold email, you might want to add a Power Statement consisting of your Value Proposition.

A value proposition is a unique selling proposition that highlights the benefits that your product or service offers. Notice that I say 'benefits' and not 'features'.

Nobody is interested in your solution's features. Your prospects are interested in what benefits they will get out of partnering with you instead of your competitor. Or remain with their status quo.

As cold emailing is about getting the foot in the door, a clear and concise value proposition can be incredibly useful in structuring your cold emails.

First, you need to find out what your prospects' most pressing problems and top challenges are.

You will find hints of that in Trigger Events and your research about your prospect's organisation. Your cold emails should then directly address these Trigger Events and offer an idea that can help them move forward (and not backward).

In essence, you will be offering value by helping to close these gaps.

Your Value Proposition is the best place to demonstrate your capabilities, your knowledge about your prospect's business situation and strategy, and highlight how you can help them achieve their goals by providing prove of what you have done with other customers and the results they achieved. More on that later.

In general, a value proposition consists of 3 parts:

1. *Business Driver*

2. *Movement*

3. *Metrics*

Business Driver

The main inputs and activities that drive a company's operational and financial results are known as business drivers. To make internal decisions about a firm strategy or construct a financial model to value a firm, you must first have an excellent grasp of the primary drivers of the business.

The drivers differ greatly by industry and have an impact on all financial aspects of a company: revenues, expenses, and capital expenditures.

It's the collection of people, circumstances, and information that start and sustain activities that will help a company define and achieve its objectives. These drivers represent the most important influences or elements for a company's success.

Every company - and industry - has their business drivers, and they can vary on a broad scale. Internal and external factors mold strategic drivers. Mission, people, and financial goals are examples of internal drivers.

External influencers include markets, competition, taxes, rules and regulations, technological developments, and customer demands. An organisation can prioritise them and devise strategies around them after they have determined the specific driving forces for their firm.

Business driver examples are:

- *Lead conversation rate*
- *Cost of goods sol*
- *Share of customer*
- *Customer retention*
- *Market share*
- *Lifetime customer value*
- *Churn rates*
- *Energy consumption*
- *Compliance*
- *Operating costs*
- *Time to profitability*
- *Breakeven*
- *Profit margins*
- *Acquisition integration*
- *Labour costs*
- *Productivity*
- *Downtimes / Uptimes*
- *Security*
- *Sales cycle*
- *Employee turnover*

Time to market

The reasons why it is important for you to incorporate business drivers in your value proposition is that it clearly relates to your prospect's pain and foundation for decision making.

Sometimes, one value proposition does not hit your prospects pain points strongly enough. You might need to try out different angles that could trigger more interest and response in your cold email.

Having more than one value proposition in your arsenal will provide you with the confidence and 'fire power'.

Movement

A business driver without a Movement is meaningless. So let's have a look at typical business driver movements for your value proposition:

- *Increase*
- *Accelerate*
- *Strengthen*
- *Shorten*
- *Cut*
- *Reduce*
- *Decrease*
- *Improve*
- *Enhance*
- *Grow*
- *Save*
- *Squeeze*
- *Balance*
- *Free up (time/resources)*
- *Eliminate*
- *Minimise*
- *Revitalise*
- *Shrink*
- *Maximise*

Metrics

Now you are going to make your value proposition tangible and irresistible by adding specific metrics to it.

Such as:

- *23%*

- *17%*

- *87%*

- *53%*

Value Proposition Example

Bringing it all together could look something like this:

We recently worked with XYZ [or: a company in your prospect's industry] on their labour costs. They achieved a 37% reduction in labour cost and a 57% faster onboarding of new hires within the first 3 months.

Once you have tailored your value proposition to your prospect's situation and deliver it with stamina and confidence, you will make you and your solution almost irresistible and impossible to ignore.

The Closing

In closing, you should include a 'Next Step' and 'Call to Action'. Avoid asking your prospects to get back to you or have them send you their availabilities for a phone call.

Be proactive and unapologetic!

A great closing of your cold email could look something like this:

- *I have some ideas on how you can [achieve xyz]. If you're interested, I can send you a link to some articles that you might find helpful.*

- *I will be in your city next week. I am happy to meet with you at a time that is good for you.*

- *Just a quick question: Would you be kind enough to point me to the person responsible for XYZ?*

- *I'll call you tomorrow at 10am. If another time suits you better, let me know*

Your Signature

Again, keep your signature simple and brief.

Your name, your company, phone number and website link. That should be it. Why is it important to keep an eye on your signature?

Number one

If your prospect does not know you, it is most likely that they will have a look at your signature to find out more before deciding whether or not to reply.

Number two

Your signature is not an extension of your cold email.

Number three

As to why you should pay close attention to your signature is because it is one of the things that prospects will look at before replying to cold emails.

Number four

It is not an ego playground for your 'big' job title.

Number five

Cold emails are not an alternative to your LinkedIn profile.

Number six

Cold emails are all about respect and effective communication, so having a professional signature - short, sweet, brief and professional - is definitely crucial here!

PS:

Should you include a PS in your email? It depends. Studies have shown that a PS is getting read without failure. So if you have something important to add, put it in the PS.

Make sure, though, that you do not exceed the 90-words limit. At least by no more than 10 words.

Yup, a really short chapter. Just like a 'PS'. ;)

Conclusion

Remember, you want your prospects to reply in two ways:

1) Yes

2) No

Both responses are valuable insights for your as a sales person. Why? Well, because any reaction is positive. Therefore, use the opportunity to get your prospect on the phone or reply to you email.

A response can come in a few different forms:

1) They reply back asking for or providing additional information

2) They completely ignore your email

3) They reply to you telling you that they are not interested in buying your product

No matter what, if someone is giving you a response, it means that they are taking the time out of their day to read your email and think about who you are and what you have to say.

A cold email is a way for you to get your foot in the door with prospective customers, but it can be hard knowing how to draft one.

To make sure that cold emails are successful and provoke responses from prospects, there are some tips we want to share. Especially if cold emails are an important part of your digital marketing strategy!

Make it personal

Personalize your cold email as much as possible so that any prospect reading will feel like they're getting something special just for them

Keep it short

Don't try and write a novel when crafting cold emails because this could come off as unprofessional or pushy

Be specific

Include details about what you're offering (and why) right up front so that it's the first thing that your cold email gets to. It will let the reader know immediately what they're getting and why it'll make their lives easier, which is exactly what you want to grab their attention

Be clear on how you can help

Don't sell them something that doesn't solve their problems or fit into their current strategy. Instead of focusing on what you can do for them, focus on how your cold email offering will help them achieve their goals and make sure that it is something they need

Keep in mind time zones

If cold emails are sent during business hours, make this clear at the top without having to look it up. Be aware of working hours so that they know when to read and respond accordingly

Lastly

The best time to send your email is 7am. So make sure you schedule your cold emails to be sent at the best time for maximum impact.

Much Success!

Josef Reisz

www.honeycombagency.co.uk

Printed in Great Britain
by Amazon